SIMPLES

KateLynn Hibbard

ALSO BY KATELYNN HIBBARD

Sleeping Upside Down

Sweet Weight

When We Become Weavers: Queer Female Poets on the Midwestern Experience (editor)

SIMPLES

KateLynn Hibbard

Winner of the 2018 Howling Bird Press Poetry Prize

HOWLING
BIRD
PRESS

Howling Bird Press
Augsburg University
2211 Riverside Avenue
Minneapolis, MN 55454

http://engage.augsburg.edu/howlingbird/

Published 2018 by Howling Bird Press
Printed in the United States of America
Cover design and photo, interior design, and typesetting by Steve Foley
The text of this book is set in Adobe Garamond Pro.

ISBN: 978-0-9961952-4-9

First Edition

18 19 20 21 22 5 4 3 2 1

This book is printed on acid-free, recycled paper.

for our grandmothers' grandmothers
and for Jan, always

CONTENTS

SIMPLES

KateLynn Hibbard

PART I

Swarm

1.

Blow ye the trumpet in Zion, and sound an alarm in my holy mountain: let all the inhabitants of the land tremble: for the day of the LORD cometh, for it is nigh at hand

This is a story about desire

Wings of golden lace
the slow knowing eyes
immense legs to power the sudden springing
Singly, in pairs, their trill says summer says barn full of hay
says barley water a day at the creek
The children catch them buzzing in their hands
A dry year, the third one running
stalks parched and brittle
the plow tearing the tight thatch of sod
to reveal dark earth turning gray in an instant
it had happened before and they knew
the rains would come again

a swarm a cloud a shadow
a hundred miles wide, a swath as big as the places the people had left
years before O pioneers, pianos and horsehair sofas,
glass windows that fit in their frames, a steady supply
of tobacco and sugar, starch for the collars
and coal in the bin
doors that shut tight against the luminous wind

For lo I contain multitudes
more than one million per mile

as bountiful as the bison
who thundered the western plains

it came out of the west
not thunderheads scudding the wide sky
not the green of a gathering twister
but something glinting around the edges
like a golden fleece their wings caught sunlight
there was no wind, the air still and hot
and the cloud moved faster than wind

*The earth shall quake before them; the heavens shall tremble: the sun and
the moon shall be dark, and the stars shall withdraw their shining*

then no more gold but darkness

2.
They make a fearful noise in their flight

rasping whirring like cart wheels over stone like flame like rain
hitting the ground the house the barn the shed the trees the fields
the fences the horses the cattle the chickens the pigs the dogs
like a blizzard of green cloaking all in their path
like thunder like a train like the running of the bison
like a blanket on the ground nearly one foot deep.

*They shall run to and fro in the city; they shall run upon the wall, they shall
climb up upon the houses; they shall enter in at the windows like a thief.*

Trees bowed over with the weight of them and they ate—
the tall grass the wheat the corn the sunflowers
the oats the barley the buckwheat the bark
of trees and the leaves of trees, linden, scrub oak, cottonwood,

willow, potato bush and onion top, pole beans, turnip leaves,
the lacy fronds of carrots, the purple stained beet greens
the blankets the women threw on the crops to protect them
fence posts sheep's wool the harnesses on horses
curtains on the windows aprons and overalls on the line
and the clothes from the back of a man who thought to stop them
by running into their thunder

3.
Before their face the people shall be much pained: all faces shall gather
blackness.

One family in ten had enough food to last the winter.
The pigs too thin to render lard
When the side pork is gone, eat greens
When the greens are gone, eat cabbage soup
When the cabbage is gone, eat nothing

This is a story about power in numbers

Those who could leave went back to the cities or west again, further still
Some went mad and died another death
Many had so little left they could not leave
Thousands remained and plowed and planted again

And thousands more poured into the prairie
seeking their golden dreams

Naming the Plants

Unbroken ocean of green. Nothing
for the eye to rest on. Everything
the same, as far as the eye
could see. Farther.

      Indian bread root, yellow star grass, golden Alexander, Seneca
      root, prairie cordgrass, prairie dropseed, big bluestem

Look closely—the flowers
and grasses are not alike. We
would do well to give them names,
as Adam gave the animals

          And out of the ground the Lord God formed every beast
          of the field, and every fowl of the air; and brought
          them unto Adam to see what he would call them: and
          whatsoever Adam called every living creature, that was
          the name thereof.

      Prairie crocus, prairie smoke, smooth fleabane, black-eyed
      Susan, yellow coneflower, meadow blazing star, low prairie rose

And what of the woman
we stayed with our first summer?
I taught her to plait her hair
like mine, to throw off her blanket
and wear a proper dress.

      Nodding ladies' tresses, small white ladyslipper

She cared for the baby while we worked our wheat,
built a bridge from willow twigs
to ford our little stream. She
was a good Indian. No, I don't recall that she had
a name. I did not record it.

Rhubarb

It is my aim to break the prairie
one pie plant at a time, from behind the barn
in Sandusky to the side of this shack
outside of Aberdeen. Acid,
tonic, it asks for a bit of sweetness,
red-veined stalks oozing juice
that pools in the bottom of the pan.

It is my aim to make the most of our bounty
such as it is and prepare for the scarceness
we know must come
hidden in this wind that will never end,
to transform what is bitter.

For roasted rhubarb, peel as for pie
and put long pieces
in the graniteware baking dish,
the one that didn't break
on the long ride from Ohio.
For two quarts rhubarb allow one
and a quarter cup sugar sprinkled over.
Bake until tender. No water is needed,
a very good thing where none
is to be had without carrying
from five miles off.

It is my aim to cure what can be cured
with the materials at hand. Astringent, aperient,
it soothes a baby's stomach ache,
makes a good wash for scrofulous sores.

For pie, pour boiling water over it,
let stand until cold and reserve the water
for lemonade made without lemons.
Blanching removes some bitterness
and allows the use of sorghum
where sugar is dear.

It is my aim to remove whatever stains.
Take half a stalk, mince it up and add a cup
of water. Boil and cool and dab the juice
on the stained blouse or what have you with a brush.
Rinse under warm water and launder as usual,
or what passes for usual in these parts.

Over time, the crowns get crowded,
and must be divided every five years,
so by the time you've proved your claim
you may take some along
to the new place. If good roots are set out,
by the second spring it will be just
in its prime, it will thrive
in new ground, its crinkled leaves
heart-shaped and deadly,
broad as the palms laid before
the Virgin Mary. Pass it on
as you go further west, that all may know
a woman's hand was here, and here, and here.

Bottle Gentian

Because you come in late summer
to wither in an August frost
or wilt with October's late fever,

your cobalt body
pleated like a fine sleeve,
a fluted tube,
a blue-faced flame,

blister beetles
gnaw your flowers.

Because you never fully open,
only the largest bees
are strong enough
to climb inside

to suck the last feast
of the season.

Closed petals clustered,
a handful of lanterns
above a strong stem.

Color of twilight
after the sun has dropped,
before the moonblack hours,
before the rustle of the coverlet,
the hand beneath the dress of night.

Because you come back
every year on winged seeds
to the rich low prairie,
to the mouth of the meadow,

your heavy yellow root
reaching deep underground
releasing your juice
to poultice our pains.

Endless bud,
you are always beginning,
sweet within
and bitter at the root.

Because you closed
your mouth,

Because you let no one else
come inside,

those who do not know you
would call you blind.

Lace

In all things familiar
she sees gossamer,
a hint of filigree in the ribs
of sliced cabbage,
spirals skirting the center
of the Queen Anne's lace
nodding its head outside
her cabin door,
pale strands twisted back
on themselves
enclosing nothing
but air,
yet with enough strands wound around,
that nothing will become something—
the lace of queens
and the queen of laces.

At the government outpost
she finds nothing at first
but a few rough buildings
with cockleburs scratching
at the doors, her cabin a homely
room with a potbellied stove,
sleeping quarters in the attic
with plenty of air holes
in walls and roof.

She sees patterns everywhere,
in the ripples

circling from a stone
thrown in the smooth glass
of the lake,
in the aura of light
around the sun,
in the kernel of rice
snug on its stem,
in the round head
of the child at the dark girl's breast,
and the fine whorl of his hair
spiraling from the center of his scalp.

Already the women can make baskets,
their mouths rounding
the emptiness of air,
they know how to shape birch bark
and sweet grass,
to weave the shell
that waits to be filled
with something.

When the women come to her
dressed in dark cotton,
their raven hair braided long
down their backs,
she worries they will soil the fine work
with their brown hands,
yet they take great pride
in the boxes of needlepoint lace
sent to the ladies in New York City—
bureau scarves and handkerchiefs,
cushion covers, collars, and cuffs
crafted from the best linen thread.

Some of the women walk from miles away
to carry on the work,
at which they are remarkably clever.

To make something out of nothing—
she takes comfort in knowing
the moral uplift
of having honest work to do
will surely lift the savage
from her lowly place.

Prairie Larkspur

Where is the royal blue queen
of my cottage garden, hollow stemmed beauty

that breaks easily in high wind,
her tall, bold blossoms the occasion
for gathering friends to tea

to admire the blue of deep water,
the blue that cooled the yellow heat

of marigold and Persian roses?
How unlike my delphinium you are!
Drooping, nodding, your flowers are pale

and powdery, the back of each one
like the thin hind toe of a bird, though

I see her shadow in your flowering spike,
the fathomless blue of a prairie sky.
Your stems erect and stout,

your tall stalks wave above the endless grasses, perhaps
not as lovely as our garden flowers

but useful to the Indians
or so I have been told, seeds
that serve for killing lice
or filling rattles, flowers pressed
to dye cloth in shades of orange and green.

No matter. If what is left to me of beauty
must be these bird-footed denizens of the plains,
so be it. Soon you too will fall beneath the plow.

To Make Baking Powder Biscuits

Gather as much of the cow wood as you can
You will use quite a lot as it burns pretty fast
First stoke the stove and then go wash your hands

Figure two or three for a fairly hungry man
You could try to make extra but the dough don't last
Gather as much of the cow wood as you can

You will need a quart of flour for every pan
Saleratus and a spoon full of butter makes the best
Stoke up the stove and wash your hands again

Cut out half a dozen with the top of the powder can
Try to piece another small one from what's left
Gather as much of the cow wood as you can

You have to keep on stoking 'til they're done
Pierce them with a broom straw first to test
Then stoke the stove and wash your hands again

And now you're done with breakfast. Plan
To start your dinner biscuits in another hour at best
So gather as much of the cow wood as you can
And stoke the stove, and wash your hands again

The Hired Man

appears in the doorway
of the milking shed, a shadow
filling the square of light,
his face obscured, his eyes
unseen. Watching her. She turns
away, keeps milking, rests
her head on Abigail's flank, listens
to her deep stomach rumble. Pulls
her teats, one, two, one, two,
rhythmic squirt of warm milk
in the pail and without warning
the stool is gone and she is sprawled
across dirty straw, the pail
upended, blue-white stream
gathering dirt as it rolls across
the cracked floor, her face pushed
into hay bales stacked
in the corner, muffled screams
withered on bitter wind, the tearing
of her muslin underskirt harsh
like an axe cleaving wood, she watches
the milk roll across the floor, when will
it end, then slow to a trickle, she prays
for God's forgiveness, knows
she will soon be punished for losing
her morning's work.

Curtains

White cambric petticoat torn from a gown,
White lace refinement on tarpaper walls,
Fashioned from newspaper, cheesecloth, and sheets,
Cut out from calico, brightened with ribbon,
Fastened with penny nails, tied back with string,
Worthy of more than this sacrificed fabric,
To make of our place a true home from sod,
Beat back the blindness that burns through our days,
Haven of shade to pull closed for the night.
As women are meant to wear dresses,
So windows are curtained, contained, defined,
To keep out the dark ones who watch us.
But what do they want, and where can we hide,
With no other shelter in sight?

PART II

Thimble

Chilocco Indian School, 1898

at first it felt clumsy
like I had grown two
extra fingers

hand stitching
the way my mother taught me
weaving the needle in and out
in a straight line
was no longer possible

In the first year: Never permit sewing without a thimble

and I couldn't figure out what to do
with my fingers
could not make them curl
just so, like a lady's hands

my hands are wide like my father's
and so are my fingers

Do not let children make knots in thread.

with no knot, my thread kept slipping out
of the needle

it was like learning to sew
all over again

All civilized nations have obtained their culture through the work of the hand assisting the development of the brain.

putting on a thimble hurts

it needs to be snug
to trap the fingers

Basketry, weaving, netting, and sewing were the steps in culture taken by primitive people.

not so tight that you need to force it on
but tight enough so it doesn't slip off
by itself

Biting threads must never be tolerated.

my thread shreds so fast

Drill in the use of the thimble, length of the thread, threading needle, motion of arm in taking stitches, fastening thread

the proper hold takes a while to get used to

we make dishtowels and pillowcases by the hundreds
practical things to be used at the school
patch and darn day after day
sew silver buttons
on pinafores and uniforms

Drill in the use of emery and holding scissors

the teachers believe we will stab ourselves
without the use of a thimble
they do not want our stain
on their needlework

Sonata Beneath the Stars

Tuck the fiddle tight beneath your chin,
high lonesome wail, a song of yelps
and moans for an audience of air.

Try an arpeggio with fingers
more accustomed to grasping
the handle of your plow.

Let coyotes treble the refrains,
and when the bow scrapes,
take resin from the limber pine,

let the sap from the living tree
seal off wounds, and at the first sign of spring
scrape the outer bark

into shapes like flying geese,
wounding the tree so the resin may flow.
To rosin your bow,

loosen and shake its hair
like the vain woman you once were,
whipping it through the snow

that still splits the Nebraska sky.
Let Orion chase the Seven Sisters,
three stars in his belt bright as a serenade.

Simples

Feverfew, fleabane, boneset, thyme,

      Dear Minnie: How are you all—I find myself alone a good deal of the time. After the loss of the wheat this third year running, Alexander has gone further west to look for work. Perhaps he will hire out on another man's claim, somewhere the hoppers haven't hit.

to restore manly vigor, sweet sarsaparilla

      These last two springs have brought us no rain, and the cabbages grow scarcely larger than a man's fist.

sassafras to cleanse the blood

      The little ones fret so with stomach pain. More than once they have gone to bed hungry.

Lydia Pinkham's vegetable tonic for woman troubles

      I manage all right by myself, though I do expect another confinement in October.

Beeswax pessary to stop a child

Cora b. 1880
Josiah b. 1881
Althea b. 1882
Camilla b. 1883
John b. 1884

if the wax fails, pennyroyal and Queen Anne's lace

I pray that I might see you again. Do not worry about us. The Lord helps those who help themselves. I remain your faithful sister, Nannie.

Egg Money

Barnes County, North Dakota, 1893

When I was to be married
my brother gave me
a small flock of laying hens,
six biddies
and a Rhode Island Red rooster.

By the next year
I was raising seventy-five chicks
such a ruckus of chirping
when I brought around pans
of water and mash!
I kept them in the kindling box
next to the cook stove
until they were old enough
to live outside,
prayed they would escape
the marauding fox.

Well, enough of them did,
and in two years' time
I walked fourteen miles
to town with a crate full of eggs
on my back, paying
for sugar and salt,
coffee and kerosene,

and I could sell a broiler
for 25 cents, got 50 cents a piece
for laying hens,

but when the government man
came through and drew up his report
on the work
done on our farm,
there was no name but my husband's—
"wheat farmer" it said
for occupation—

no mention of the stacked eggs
packed in straw,
feathered carnage by the back shed,
no name for the plucking,
the singeing of skin
to ease out the feathers,

no word for my labor but wife.
Mother. Helpmeet.

The Bruise

Nothing more
than the release
of blood beneath
the skin, the bruise
will surely fade
in three weeks' time.
She made me
a poultice
of comfrey
to reduce the
swelling, said
it would help
heal tissue
and bone, said
a handful of
parsley crushed
would clear up
the black and blue
marks in a
day or two.
She did not say
what I might do
if he comes back
from the saloon
in such a state
again, though
St. John's Wort
has worked wonders
for some, and
I found that to be
a bit more

comfort than
the preacher's counsel
to abide by my
wifely duties
without further
ado.

Juneberry

Late March and the land still crouches
on winter haunches, waiting
for a sign of thaw. In the root cellar,
she pulls down the last dusty jar
of juneberries,

remembers the day last summer
taking her children to the river
where the shrubs grow thick
with the sweet, small,
blue-black jewels.

She can still see Sarah's lips
stained purple, hears herself scold the child
to put more fruit in the bucket.

The Dakota woman who showed her
where to find them called it medicine berry,
said when eaten raw it will purify
the blood.

Precious little sugar left to squander
on a kuchen, they will eat these few
with molasses and cream
if any will come from the gaunt-sided cow.

When the juneberry bush blossoms,
surely the frost will have left the ground soft enough
to bury the winter's dead.

She pries the lid quickly, not wanting to see
the wan child turning her face from the spoon,
too weak with fever to cry.

Through My Window I See a Vision of My Mother,

Who gave me over to this world of men
And fields subdued by wild October winds,
Whose face I may not live to see again
If these preserves don't last until the spring.

Mother, I drink my coffee weak and cold.
You taught me not to want much, yet I plead
Beneath low skies foretelling months of snow
For strength like yours. You gave me to believe

That God knows where we are and cares to save
All souls that perish, pummeled as the wheat
Is by the rain. What good is it to grieve
The force that stripped my child away from me?

My daughter. What was left for her to see?
What window to look through, if not through me?

Indian Boarding School Memories

This poem is based on remarks by Omaha tribal elder Elsie Gilpin Morris on her experiences at the Genoa U.S. Indian School in Nebraska in the 1930s.

She couldn't eat. All she did was cry
For hours on the train to Genoa.
She got lost from her sister
In the dime store at Fremont.

It took hours on the train to Genoa.
They cut Elsie's braids
After the dime store at Fremont,
Before they assigned her bed.

They cut Elsie's braids.
She didn't know a word of English.
Before they assigned her bed,
They put kerosene on her head.

Elsie didn't know a word of English.
It burned her eyes.
They put kerosene on her head,
Took her clothes away.

It burned her eyes.
Elsie had new shoes, was so proud of them.
They took her clothes away,
And she never saw them again.

Elsie had new shoes, was so proud of them.
They required dresses of striped denim,

And she never saw her shoes again.
Her pantaloons only had one button,

Under dresses made of striped denim.
Elsie's first grade teacher had red hair,
And pantaloons sporting more than one button.
She was Chippewa from Minneapolis.

Elsie's first grade teacher had red hair,
Her name was Miss McDougal.
Said she was Chippewa from Minneapolis.
She would write on the board

"My name is Miss McDougal"
The children repeated English after her.
She wrote on the board
All that summer,

The children repeated English after her.
Their folks couldn't bring them home
In the summer.
On Sundays Elsie had free time.

Her folks couldn't bring her home.
But she said it wasn't too bad.
On Sundays Elsie had free time
So she had to clean the building.

She said it wasn't too bad. With her friends
She stole cherries, hid them in her dress.
Elsie had to clean the building.
The matron was waiting for her.

She hid stolen cherries in her dress
But didn't get to eat a one.
The matron was waiting for her.
Pinched apples in her socks,

And she didn't get to eat a one.
Elsie lost her shoes in the mud,
Pinched apples in her socks.
They told her not to go to Beaver Creek

Elsie lost her shoes in the mud.
The matron said,
"I told you not to go to Beaver Creek—
No supper."

The matron said,
"Pick out your stick.
No supper."
There was a board, a ruler, a switch.

"Pick out your stick."
Elsie told the other girls in her language,
(There was a board, a ruler, a switch)
"Scream and holler as loud as you can."

Elsie told the other girls in her language
At home, Omaha children were never hit.
"Scream and holler as loud as you can!"
The girl who picked the switch had welts.

At home, Omaha children were never hit.
When the school closed Elsie had to go home.

The girl who picked the switch had welts.
She traveled back in an open truck.

When the school closed Elsie had to go home.
Her father said I'm glad you're home.
She traveled back in an open truck
I hated to send you there—

Her father said I'm glad you're home
It hurts my heart—
I hated to send you there—
But knew you needed to learn their ways.

It hurts my heart.
I hope you have not lost your words.
I knew you needed to learn their ways.
Elsie practiced Omaha every Sunday

She had lost some of her words.
After she got home it seemed like
She practiced Omaha every Sunday.
She could never get her hair to grow again.

After Elsie got home it seemed like
She got lost from her sister.
She could never get her hair to grow again.
She couldn't eat. All she did was cry.

Uses for Salt

To remove mildew from linen, moisten the spot with salt and soap, place out in the sun until stain is removed.

When I was married, the older women, they used Vaseline a lot.

To remove tea stains on cups, rub salt on spots.

They said a greased egg wouldn't hatch.

To prevent bluing from streaking clothes, put a handful of salt in last rinsing water.

And then of course we were more or less a little bit careful.

It will also keep them from sticking to the line on a frosty day.

I suppose the Catholics called it the rhythm.

To make a candle burn longer, fill with salt around the wick, up to the blackened part.

We were told as long as you nursed a baby you wouldn't conceive.

Remedy for colic—dissolve one teaspoonful each salt and black pepper (ground) in a glass of cold water. Drink as much as possible and lie down. Repeat the dose if necessary.

And then a lot of them used salt.

To remove ink stains, salt is good for carpets or woolen goods.

The kind they put in ice cream. Rock salt.

Cover the stain and let stand a few minutes then brush off lightly and add clean salt and brush vigorously.

I never did use the rock salt.

In most cases the stain will disappear.

We were told it affected the mind.

To prevent hair from falling out—put two tablespoons full of salt on paper and with a stiff brush dipped in it rub the scalp.

There was a lady that come through one time, and she had a receipt.

A dash of salt improves the taste of coffee.

She took cocoa butter and boric acid.

Clean brass, copper, and pewter with paste made of salt and vinegar, thickened with flour.

And you made these little cones and you'd use those.

Soak stained handkerchiefs in salt water before washing.

We made them together.

Sprinkle salt on your shelves to keep ants away.

Oh yes, it worked.

Wild Rose Elixir

You will need a nice glass jar
and your best friend Frieda to walk with you
to Painted Woods Creek
to "gather ye rosebuds while ye may,"
and you will need Shana's recipe—
the one she carried with her
from Kresilev to Grand Forks—
and you will need
some of Uncle Noah's vodka,
enough to fill the jar three quarters full,
and honey enough to fill the rest.

Each day before the Sabbath
for six weeks' time,
you must shake that jar
and wait.

When it is done, strain
into another jar
and take some to Sarah
who almost fainted last year
from raking hay
in the blazing sun.
Give a little to Sophie to use
before she steps into the mikvah
her husband built her on their farm.
And save a sip to share
with Micah, the proprietor's son
from the general store,
to open his heart
so one day he will marry you.

PART III

Wound Medicine

1.

Do you remember, I wrote you of a little baby boy dying?

Red skin, the baby burning, screaming at her touch.

He was such a sweet, beautiful boy.

Bright red butterfly of rash
across the bridge of his nose, his cheeks
hot, the skin shiny and swollen and hard.

Cranberries raw and mashed fine, made into a poultice is said
to cure it.

For a long time my heart was crushed.

They grow low and viney. You see them back home in the
spring, flowers light pink and splayed back, lolling their long
red tongues.

Cranberries, down in the swampy spots
in the wet woods of Wisconsin.

She was trained as a nurse. She had seen this before, one lesion
hard and distinct, then more, like coals catching,
joining and spreading without stopping.

The Ojibwe knew where to find them, put them
in pemmican, wound medicine, dye.

The infection flames like a wave beneath the skin

hand-picked, one at a time come autumn,
cranberries like red drops of blood.

Beloved, let us love one another, for love is of God;
and everyone that loveth is born of God, and
knoweth God.

St. Anthony's Fire.

the skin of the berry firm around its pocket of air.

2.

As there was no physician, there was no priest to comfort

By night his eyes swelled shut
and she was grateful
not to see
his eyes anymore.

There is no fear in love. But perfect love casteth out fear:
because fear hath torment. He that feareth is not made perfect
in love.

He died of erysipelas.

stems dark and slender,
sometimes near a stream. In the lowlands.

I held him in my arms till the last agony was over.

She felt his body stiffen and writhe,
stiffen and writhe, watched
the light move across

the stove, the chair, the jar
of rabbit brush stuck in the window

3.

      not much grows at this altitude, no wet-
      lands for miles, just

           Then I dressed the beautiful little body for the grave.

      stinkweed and spider flower

           Clyde is a carpenter; so I wanted him to make
           the little coffin.

      pinyon pine, Rocky Mountain maple

           I lined and padded it, trimmed and covered it.

      As the Father hath loved Me, so have I loved you: continue
      ye in My love.

           I selected a chapter from John

      Ye are of God, little children, and have overcome them:
      because greater is he that is in you, than he that is in the
      world.

           It was a sad pleasure to do everything ourselves.

           That was my own little Jamie, our first little son.

Spirit House

White Earth Indian Agency, 1895

1.
The first year I did not know how much of the Burial Service to read—
"Every word" was Bishop Morrison's reply.

> *MAN, that is born of a woman, hath but a short time to live, and*
> *is full of misery. He cometh up, and is cut down, like a flower; he*
> *fleeth as it were a shadow, and never continueth in one stay.*

I knew Sarah's time was coming, saw
the other Chippewa women help her choose
the garments she would wear
in the next life:
a robe of crimson silk
with much lace and many ribbons,
a wreath of artificial flowers,
white silk stockings with white kid slippers,
white gloves for her poor little hands.

> *In the midst of life we are in death: of whom may we seek for*
> *succour, but of thee, O Lord, who for our sins art justly displeased?*

I saw the dying woman's pleasure:
unwrapping each package from the mail order house
sending for a pine box padded and lined
in white sateen, a white marble stone
to be placed on her grave,
preparing to meet her Creator

Yet, O Lord God most holy, O Lord most mighty, O holy and
most merciful Saviour, deliver us not into the bitter pains of
eternal death.

2.
As there was no priest or deacon
and none were allowed to visit
for fear of smallpox

     Thou knowest, Lord, the secrets of our hearts

I prepared to read the Burial Service
as I had done many times by now
sometimes standing in snow to my knees.

     shut not thy merciful ears to our prayer; but spare us, Lord most
     holy, O God most mighty, O holy and merciful Saviour;

I considered my own poor garments
the tattered dress, stockings that needed darning,
wondered at the extravagance
lavished on Sarah's lifeless clay
far beyond her family's means

     thou most worthy Judge eternal
     suffer us not, at our last hour, for any pains of death, to fall
     from thee.

Soon Sarah's grave will be covered with wood,
two feet high and the length of the casket,
with a wee round hole for escape of the spirit
and a shelf for offerings to refresh the departed.

FORASMUCH as it hath pleased Almighty God, in his wise
providence to take out of this world the soul of our deceased sister,
we therefore commit her body to the ground;

First fruits of the harvest will be brought here

> *earth to earth,*
> *ashes to ashes*
> *dust to dust;*

most of it devoured by birds and other denizens of the wild
and sometimes by the children

3.

> *looking for the general Resurrection in the last day, and the life of*
> *the world to come, through our Lord Jesus Christ;*

Sarah's pagan friends will build a fire
for three nights so her soul may suffer
no hardship from cold and darkness
on its three-day journey to its final resting place

> *at whose second coming in glorious majesty to judge the world, the*
> *earth and the sea shall give up their dead;*

Mrs. Wiswell will play the organ and the Indians will sing,
Christian hymns having long replaced
the Chippewa women's wailing.
Those saved by God shall sing to Him:
"The strife is o'er, the battle done
the victory of life is won;
the song of triumph has begun:
Alleluia!"

and the corruptible bodies of those who sleep in Him shall be changed and made like unto His own glorious body; according to the mighty working whereby He is able to subdue all things unto Himself.

Braucher

The first time they sent for me
it was to treat the youngest child
who suffered a fortnight with stomachache.
I tied a string around her belly three times,
then took that string and tied it around an egg.

From Wurtemberg to Volga,
from Volga to North Dakota,
for poultice and salve,
to pack their boils with salt
and cabbage leaves,
to steep tea of valerian
for the sweetest sleep—

ich brauche dich! they cry.
When all else fails
they come to me.

Father Miller wants
to cast me away
from his church,
but I am no witch—
and I have used my gifts
far longer than he,
like my mother did
and her mother before her.

Of course without God
there is no healing,
so you must throw that egg in the fire
while saying the prayer

that casts out the pain—
Gott der Vatte
Gott der Sohn
Gott der Heilige Geist.

The Itch

We must have picked it up
at school last winter,
likely from that Taylor family
just moved here from DeSmet,
from the looks of those brats
they haven't had a bath
since New Year's.

My sister has it on both wrists,
and in between her fingers.
Mine is worst along my waistline—
they call it the seven-year itch
and if it lasts that long
I do believe I may lose all sense.

Have we been smitten with
the botch of Egypt? In Bible study
the preacher warned of the scab and the itch,
whereof thou canst not be healed.

Ma rubbed us with sulphur and grease
and turned us like a couple of roasting hens
in front of the fire
and still we had an awful time.

Night after night I could feel them
burrowing into my skin
and finally she called for the braucher.

For fire beneath the skin,
she prayed over our bodies

while making the sign of the cross three times,
so the heat would rise and follow her.
Then she bathed us both in flour
and the holy spirit and promises
that our skin will soon be clear.

Root Cellar

West Point, Nebraska, November 1868

1.
When the rain finally stopped I had hoped for some peace
but it was not to be. Fierce gales from the north
blew the siding right off the shack and by the time
I picked it up in the yard my fingers had started to freeze.

Put my hands in cold water. Three days later they still burn.

Slept poorly in the storm, thinking of Lewis
gone to town for supplies, and woke to my bed
nearly covered in snow. The wood
about gone and too windy to go out
for more. I dare not venture as far as the shed
to feed chickens and hog, hope the Lord spares them
to us, poor dumb beasts.

2.
A pan of hot coals, a lamp
and a candle and the blessed Word.
The chair won't fit through the trap door
but the bedding is easy enough to push
down to the root cellar.

Dug so deep in the earth
it will not freeze, this burrow and the Lord
my only hope for survival.

It grows colder. Carrots bunched like fists
reach for me as I sit up and work on a muffler

for Lewis, indigo blue like his dear eyes,
knitting until I am too tired
to throw another stitch, then put all my trust
in our Heavenly Father,
knowing that he cares for us
and does all things well.

"Thou canst rebuke the storm, Thou canst
return him in safety."

Thy will be done, amen.

3.
The wind lulls and the storm has abated.
The hog is alive and very hungry.
Lewis came home and we slept together
in the cellar, nestled like potatoes in a bin.
Today he has taken out snow from our house
all day long, bushel upon bushel,
the house too cold for work
of any kind. The Lord is our only comfort,
and in him I trust.

The Fix

Uriah had been gone a good three weeks
when she started to think
she might be in a fix. Again. Already
there were the other two babes
and no work for him, accounting for
his month-long trip to Grove City.

He wrote back, said don't stay with your folks
in Minnesota too long. You might use
some other mild medicine
but nothing very strong.

The braucher said tansy tea
would be best. You will likely find some
growing along the roadside.
Steep together its bright yellow buttons
and jagged leaves until the camphor smell
almost overcomes you.

And she had heard of two women
who died drinking it. Folks said
they took it for the hysteria
but everyone knew
what that meant.

Take a cup in the morning
and another at night
while fasting
until you are healed
of your affliction.

She looked at her sleeping children,
held the cup to her lips.

Orthography, 1895

Before we came to Kansas, girls like me
had to feign being vain. I spend all day
on the claim, drive horses like a teamster.
Miss Sims says my prospects have been razed, but
this place is in my veins. I'm up before
the sun's rays pass the weather vane, fain to
beat any man at my trade. When harvest
keeps me from Sabbath, the fields are my fane.

Present Fashions of Dress

All dress must transact its weighty work, changing
old modes and boldly innovating thought and intellect
to render it progress. Our present fashions
of feminine attire are in harmony
with the swiftness and force
of a rushing cataract, stirring society
to its foundations.

Women talk eagerly on sexual equality
and a parity of pursuits among men,
which makes us see beauty and grace
in billowy clouds over thick ribs of steel.
It is good sense to attempt a revolution
against the ruling power, to modify
the caprices of costume to allow women
to transform themselves to the masculine
in harmony with feminine feeling.
And thus may it ever be.

First Night: The New Teacher

Custer County, Nebraska, 1884

She tries to dream of eiderdown
and counterpane, four-poster bed
with her trunk full of dresses at the foot,
a chair to sit at while buttoning her boots,
fresh pitcher of clean water and no ice
to break, room to stretch and roll
in the morning before sitting up
to fix her hair. Here the table
for writing letters, here the closet
full of petticoats, here
the night stand with silver brush
and comb and mirror.

So tired she can barely move
and yet she cannot sleep,
she shifts on a lumpy mattress stuffed
with heaven knows what, studies
by moonlight the face of the young girl
who shares her bed, greasy braid
coming undone, grimy fist drawn up
to her mouth, lips slightly parted
in dream. A muslin curtain
all that keeps them apart

from the snores of the hired man, weary
from his day at the plow, his name
some Scandinavian one she can't
recall, is it Sven? his thick neck

blushing red that night as he slipped
behind the curtain dividing their room.

She marvels at the sound
of a young man sleeping, wonders
what her comportment teacher would think
to see her now, hears his breath
grow quiet and sweet and pictures herself
by his side, her thick brown braid loosened
and splayed across plump pillows,
his stubble shaved clean and fingernails
white, the way he would reach for her
and clasp her hand to his lips
before resting his palm on her hip,
drawing her close to press himself
beneath the cambric nightdress
and do what she is not quite sure

but certainly something she should not
be thinking about at this very moment,
with the new school year about to start.
She lets herself down to sleep
on the ladder of his even breathing,
wonders how she will face
their intimacy in the morning,
lets her breath mingle with his
and float up into the night.

Elizabeth's Piano

When Father bought it for me
I was barely ten years old.
He got it secondhand in New York City,
but to me it was the most beautiful instrument
in the world, square and sturdy oak
with lords and ladies at tea
painted on the front to inspire
my melodies, and I practiced faithfully,
preferring my arpeggios
to all other playthings.

Shortly after I turned seventeen,
he made a shocking announcement:
we were moving to the Minnesota Territory.
Mother said we are not going
without Elizabeth's piano, and so it was
that all of us and all of our belongings
were trundled onto a riverboat,
down the turbulent Ohio, bound for Cairo.

The men who moved our things
to the next boat bound upstream
were green, did not know how
to handle anything larger than barrels
and crates, and they dropped her
into the water. Such a thunder
of wild and broken singing!
With ropes and many oaths
and groans they hauled her back on board
and off we went again, up the Mississippi

to Prescott, up the St. Croix
and overland by coach to Lakeland.

Despite that dip in the river,
the piano could still be played,
and play I did, "Child of the Angel Wing," "Susanna,"
"La Sylphide, Fantasie Romantique,"
my father having decreed music
a suitable pastime for young ladies
such as myself
who had no flax or wool to spin.

A good horse was important,
but a piano was worth twice as much,
and mine was the first many people had seen
in those parts. Soon I had students
who ferried across the river
from Hudson. One was a shy young man
who promised to tune my piano
in return for lessons.

Water makes the sound board swell,
and the pitch had gone sharper
and sharper. I had begun to despair
of ever hearing it true again,
but Carl had a gift, the sleight of hearing,
to know how much one note
could borrow from another
to reach equal temperament.
And so it was we came to play together,
"What Are the Wild Waves Saying?"
and "Come Where My Love Lies Dreaming."

PART IV

Some Rules for Teachers

From her bedroom window she watches him,
the only beekeeper in Lincoln County,
tending wooden hives set up on stilts
in the apple orchard, careful
not to crowd his colony
lest they migrate to a hollow tree
in a distant field.

> *You may not marry during the term of your contract.*
> *You are not to keep company with men.*

Sweetness spills from the cracks
of her dreams, the house loud
with humming, buzzing, waiting
for a letter from her sweetheart in Minot,
waiting for her life to begin.

Never a woman's work to tend
the bees, only to sell honey, the few
customers fiercely guarded, sun in a jar
to lighten the sting of long winters
on the edge of the prairie

> *You may not dress in bright colors.*

By day she teaches the children
of hard luck farmers and traveling preachers,
their shoes scuffed and worn,
dresses made over from their mothers'
dresses, knickers patched at the knee,
some patched at the patches.

Some eager to learn their numbers
and letters, some so far behind
from working the fields, sure to become
food for powder in the Great War.

> *You must wear at least two petticoats.*
> *Your dresses must not be any shorter than two inches above*
> *the ankle.*

Every year a new school, forced to board
with whoever lives closest.

She barely hears the creaks and groans,
pays no mind when the parlor wall
crinkles in tiny webs

Soon to be a spinster at twenty-seven,
she dreams of marriage,
a house in town. The ache in her arms
holding other people's children.

> *You may under no circumstances dye your hair.*

One small crack grows slowly,
splits open faded wallpaper roses,
the whole wall packed with the industry of bees,
waxy combs from floor to ceiling.

The children swarm to scoop up
what oozes to the wooden floor,
their small chapped hands sticky and glistening.

The Prairie of Her Body

1.

I see my future in my sister's face.
Five years of pioneering carved their scars—
A shadow of the girl in her embrace—
Five children at her side born in four years,

And one that died for lack of mother's milk.
She cried with me to see my troubled eyes,
Her skin was hardened with the sun, and dark,
A mirror like no looking glass's lies.

Her shoulders caved from bending to the babes,
The only plot her husband had to till.
No harvest after last year's locust plague,
But still the children come as though unwilled.

And I will join her soon in heading west,
The prairie of my body fading fast.

2.

The prairie of her body faded fast.
After he beat and used her for his need,
After he beat their son until he passed,
After he brought that woman to their bed,

She got their quarter section and a plow,
The house, the chairs, the wooden spoons, and plates,
The buggy, harrow, harness, and a cow,
Two colts, four horses, and a sulky rake.

She left him with his bedding, took a drill,
The pleasure that she knew the farm would bring
With next year's harvest, kept a fanning mill,
Until the time for planting in the spring,

An anvil and a hundred dollars each
For two girls she had kept safe from his reach.

3.

With our five girls, we kept safe from harm's reach
The Badlands place we'd bought before the boom
And made a decent living from the ranch
Until the day he walked out of this room.
A trip to bid on horses in Cheyenne,
He got as far as Dunn and disappeared.
If by God's will or by the will of man
I had no time to wonder. After years

Of raising girls on venison and pies
Of wild chokecherry, sometimes saskatoon,
And selling eggs and butter, and the days
I took in neighbor's wash when mine was done,

They say that life is hard without a man,
But with no husband, still I kept my land.

4.

Without my husband, I would quit this land.
After I lost the child he promised me
Never another winter would I spend
Here, where nothing grows so well as grief.

He kept his promise, built a house in town,
And every fall we move out with the cold.
A lesser man would leave me there alone,
But with him I will grow as close to old

As God has planned for me, which isn't much.
When bedtime comes he likes to brush my hair
One hundred strokes with Grandma's silver brush.
For his good sake, I pray to show no fear

When my time comes to bear another child
And make my final peace to leave this world.

5.

She had to make her peace within this world—
A small sod house divided by a wall,
A plank floor and a roof made out of wood
And on the other side, the horses' stall.

Although the house would always smell of barn
And turn a brighter green when summer came,
The horses' bodies kept her children warm
All winter. When the prairie turned to flame

And burned frame houses, they escaped the fire.
The year a brutal drought destroyed the corn
And parched the wheat, the sod stayed cool inside.
She daubed the chinks with clay. The girls took turns

To chase the mice and sweep away the grime
That fell into their food from time to time.

6.

It fell to her to make the food last, times
The locusts took their harvest and their cash.
The men would fire their guns into the swarm
And plant again, and watch the fledglings hatch.

She fed them what her garden could afford,
Potatoes and preserves and castor beans,
Five years they'd plant again and pray to God
That they would be provided with the means

To prove up. She would watch the wagons leave
With those who didn't make it in retreat
Or headed further west. She craved release,
But knew they could not pay their passage east

And had to plant again and take a stand,
Prepared to die while fighting to the end.

7.

Some prairies die. They fought it to the end,
The plague that flew in clouds like blackened sails,
But with the summer fallows came the wind
To fill their houses to the window sills

With harvest of their labor at the plow.
The good black earth that for one thousand years
Was bound by roots of prairie grass and flower,
When sown in wheat began to disappear

As cyclones raged and tore apart the land
And spread the loosened soil across the sky.
Accustomed by their faith they learned to bend
Their will to God's and not to ask Him why

The body of their prairie fell from grace.
I see my future in my sister's face.

Hanging Tree

Now that she has made up her mind,
a calm descends. The peace that passeth
all understanding. Don't think about God.
After the clothes are shaken out, the last
of the cabbage made into soup, what
is there left to look at? A table, two chairs
and a bed.

To walk five miles at a quickish pace
on a groomed trail without a break
(and wearing good shoes) would take
about a hundred minutes. This is not
that walk. The ground slick
with hoppers. Smoke rising from the fields
where the fools tried to catch them in pans
of burning oil. The tatters of what used to be
her garden. The patched, shabby boots.

She stops to rest awhile and the irony
is not lost on her. If there were a tree
on the horizon, one could judge the passing
of time but she has no tree, just time.

In the high rocky hills, she knows she could find
pine. Below that, bur oak, green ash,
white elm. On lower ground, linden
or basswood, any number of willows:
peach-leaf, river-bank, slender, or diamond.
In the deep cool ravines, balsam poplar
or paper birch. For gullies, not much
but scrub cedar.

She walks on, scans the flat horizon. Down to the river,
down to the water, down to where the trees
are sure to grow strong enough. Cottonwoods shake
their hair out over the muddy trickle below.

For a loop, the hem around her skirt will likely do.
A tear started along the seam should make easy work
of that. Still, it must be strong enough to hold her weight,
which is now a good deal less than it is about to become.
She likes to take care of things. She likes to get things done.

We Gave Up

After we lost all the wheat and the beans
The year we ate boiled grass and weeds
When they gave us a dollar for next year's seed
But none to eat turnips today
   The needy should be taught self-reliance.

After we buried two children
After the fire took our barn
After the grasshoppers came
Four years running
   If anybody chooses to lie down and be eaten up by grasshoppers, we
   don't care much if he is devoured body, boots, and breeches.

When we skimmed six bushels from the stream
In less than an hour

During the fifth year of drouth
After the first cow died
While starvation stared us in the face
   Poverty and deprivation are incidents of frontier life at its best.

Before taking the pauper's oath
Before swearing we had nothing
To qualify for succor
   It is humiliating to have them so constantly before us, passing
   round the hat.

When our neighbors got ten pounds of pork
To last the six of them all year long
   demoralization of a class fully capable of self-support

When our pigs froze in the blizzard
The year the snow flew sideways
  The lack of supplies exists chiefly among the immigrants.

When they said if we just worked hard enough
We could get rid of the grasshoppers

Because burning the earth wouldn't stop them
Because their eggs are known to survive
Even the bitterest winter
  Pluck and perseverance meet with their just reward in the saving of
  their crops by those who exercise it.

Before we gave up the last cow
Before we gave up the team and our means to plow

After they said we had too much
To deserve any help
We gave up our claim

But not without a fight

NOTES

"Swarm"

Italicized lines are from the Bible, various verses.

The poem is inspired by an article in *The Writer's Almanac,* which reads in part, "On July 20, 1875, the largest recorded swarm of locusts in American history descended upon the Great Plains. It was a swarm about 1,800 miles long, 110 miles wide, from Canada down to Texas . . . . People said the locusts descended like a driving snow in winter. They . . . blanketed the ground, nearly a foot deep . . . and ate nearly every piece of living vegetation in their path."

"Naming the Plants"

Italicized lines are from Genesis 2:19.

The woman's story is based on an incident described in Barbara Handy-Marchello's *Women of the Northern Plains: Gender and Settlement on the Homestead Frontier, 1870–1930* (St. Paul: Minnesota Historical Society Press, 2005).

"Bottle Gentian"

Blind Gentian is a related species of gentian, and the name is frequently used interchangeably with Bottle Gentian. Another name for this flower is Cloistered Heart.

"Lace"

Details from a manuscript of Pauline Colby's reminiscences on file at the Minnesota Historical Society: Pauline Colby was an Episcopal missionary and teacher sent to the White Earth and Leech Lake Indian Reservations to teach the Ojibwe women lacemaking. The project was intended to contribute to the "moral uplift" of the women, and to give them a source of income to supplement subsistence living and aid in their assimilation to white ways.

"To Make Baking Powder Biscuits"

"Cow wood" is another term for buffalo chips, dried buffalo manure, the fuel source most readily at hand on the mostly treeless prairie.

"Saleratus" is an older term for baking powder.

"Thimble"
Text in italics is from the Uniform Course of Study prescribed by
Estelle Reel, Superintendent of Indian Schools, 1898–1910.

"Simples"
Most family medicine chests contained a variety of dried herbs called
"simples"; frontier women used them to cure and treat a variety of
illnesses and complaints.

"The Bruise"
St. John's Wort has long been used for a variety of ailments, including,
in the late 1800s, hysteria and nervous imbalances with depression, as
well as alcohol cravings.

"Indian Boarding School Memories"
Genoa was an Indian boarding school in Nebraska, circa 1880–1934.
This poem is based on a talk at "Legacies and Landmarks of the
Plains Native Americans," a 2012 summer seminar hosted by Central
Community College in Columbus, Nebraska, and sponsored by the
National Endowment for the Humanities. Omaha tribal elder Elsie Gilpin
Morris, who had been a student at the Genoa U.S. Indian School, shared
memories of her experiences at the school with seminar participants.

"Uses for Salt"
Italicized lines are quoted from "Women as Workers, Women as
Civilizers: True Womanhood in the American West" by Elizabeth
Jameson (*Frontiers* 1984, vol. 7 no. 3).

Some of the home remedies and receipts (an archaic term for recipes)
are from an undated receipt book (probably early 1900s) in the author's
possession and an undated clipping from *Furrow*, an agricultural
publication.

"Wild Rose Elixir"
A mikvah is a pool of water in which observant married Jewish women
are required to immerse themselves for ritual purity. The poem is based

on incidents described in Linda Mack Schloff's *"And Prairie Dogs Weren't Kosher": Jewish Women in the Upper Midwest Since 1855* (St. Paul: Minnesota Historical Society Press, 1996).

"Wound Medicine"

Italicized lines are from a 1912 letter by Elinore Pruitt Stewart in *Letters of a Woman Homesteader* (Lincoln: University of Nebraska Press, 1989).

The remedy for erysipelas is from an undated receipt book (probably early 1900s) in the author's possession. Bible verses are from 1 John.

"Spirit House"

Based on reminiscences of Pauline Colby, an Episcopal missionary and teacher sent to the White Earth and Leech Lake Indian Reservations to teach the Ojibwe women lacemaking. The project was intended to contribute to the "moral uplift" of the women, and to give them a source of income to supplement subsistence living while helping them to assimilate to white ways. Details are from a manuscript of Colby's reminiscences on file at the Minnesota Historical Society.

Words in italics are from the Episcopal Burial Service, *1892 Book of Common Prayer.*

In her manuscript, Colby conflated aspects of Christian funerary practices with her account of Ojibwe customs: "the friends of the departed, if they chance to be still pagan, build a fire for three successive nights so that the soul may suffer no hardship from cold and darkness on its three days' journey to its final resting place." In Ojibwe tradition the spirit journey was actually four rather than three days.

"Braucher"

Brauchers are herbalists and faith healers who still practice their craft today among communities of Germans from Russia in North Dakota (Stan Stelter, "Brauche: Healing Gift Still Used by Germans," *Bismarck Tribune,* February 16, 1982).

"The Itch"

Inspired by an episode of scabies recalled in Laura Ingalls Wilder's autobiography, *Pioneer Girl* (ed. Pamela Smith Hill, Pierre, SD: South Dakota Historical Society Press, 2014).

"Root Cellar"

Based on journal entries of Martha Janney, in *900 Miles from Nowhere: Voices from the Homestead Frontier* (Steven Kinsella, St. Paul: Minnesota Historical Society Press 2006).

"The Fix"

In an 1887 letter, Uriah W. Oblinger advised his wife on how to deal with her unplanned pregnancy. From *Prairie Settlement: Nebraska Photographs and Family Letters, 1862–1912,* collection in the Library of Congress American Memory Project.

"Orthography, 1895"

Orthography refers to the art of writing with "proper" spelling and word usage. The poem is based on a question from the eighth-grade comprehensive exam given in Salinas, Kansas, in 1895: "Use the following correctly in sentences: fane, fain, feign, vane, vain, vein, raze, raise, rays."

"Present Fashions of Dress"

An erasure poem based on *Godey's Lady's Book,* Sarah J. Hale: "Editor's Table," May 1868. The original manuscript is transcribed online by Hope Greenberg, University of Vermont, December 2015.

Godey's Lady's Book, published and widely distributed from 1830–1878, is a well-known example of prescriptive literature for women. *Godey's* was best known for its advice articles and illustrations of fashion and holiday entertaining. This "Editor's Table" advised women not to embrace "unwomanly modes of thought" by transforming themselves into a "semblance of men"—advice that was not likely to be heeded by women working claims on the prairie.

"Elizabeth's Piano"

Based on "The Biography of a Piano" (Willis H. Miller, *Minnesota History Magazine,* Fall 1938) and "Pride of the Pioneer's Parlor: Pianos in Early Minnesota" (Donald C. Holmquist, *Minnesota History Magazine,* Winter 1965).

"Some Rules for Teachers"

Italicized lines are from 1915 rules for Minnesota teachers. Based on an incident described in *Florence* by Audrey K. Wendland (Edina, MN: Beaver's Pond Press, 2004).

"The Prairie of Her Body"
Sections 1 through 5 are based on women described in Barbara Handy-Marchello's *Women of the Northern Plains: Gender and Settlement on the Homestead Frontier, 1870–1930* (St. Paul: Minnesota Historical Society Press, 2005).

"Hanging Tree"
Based on a line from a short story by Mari Sandoz, as described by Sheryll Patterson-Black in "Women Homesteaders on the Great Plains Frontier" (*Frontiers*, Spring 1976).

"We Gave Up"
Italicized lines 1 through 5 are found in Annette Atkins, *Harvest of Grief: Grasshopper Plagues and Public Assistance in Minnesota, 1873–1878* (St. Paul: Minnesota Historical Society Press, 2003) and were quoted from, respectively, Senator Joseph H. Clark of Dodge County, Minnesota; *Saint Paul Pioneer Press* (May 1877); John S. Pillsbury, Governor of Minnesota, 1876–1882; a report in the *Martin County Sentinel* on New Yorkers' attitudes toward Midwesterners' ongoing pleas for relief; Governor Pillsbury, on his views about state aid for farmers. Italicized lines 6 and 7 are found in Jeffrey A. Lockwood, *Locust: The Devastating Rise and Mysterious Disappearance of the Insect that Shaped the American Frontier* (New York: Basic Books, 2004) and were quoted from Kansas historian F.W. Giles (1886) and *Saint Paul Pioneer Press* (1877).

ACKNOWLEDGMENTS

I've been working on this project for over twelve years, and so many people have helped me on this long journey to making it a book. Special thanks go to:

Hedgebrook, for the residency where the first poem, "Swarm," was drafted in 2005.

Frank X Walker, whose Split Rock Arts class in 2006 gave me courage to conjure the voices of ancestors.

My monthly writing group: Rondi Atkin, Rita Schweiss, and Morgan Grayce Willow, who have seen many of these poems in varying states and who have sustained me over the years with edits, encouragement, and pastry.

Mr. Dang at RCKT Tattoo, whose artistic rendering of my grasshopper tattoo was the magic I needed to finish the book.

The Howling Bird Press editorial team—Jim Cihlar, who is a poet's dream editor and a paragon of patience, precision, and good humor; Jannet Walsh for her brilliant website guidance; Diana Lopez Jones for her insightful editorial comments; Sharon Sobatta for creating the podcast; Ciara Hall for marketing assistance; Gabe Benson for design work; and Colin Mustful, who, along with intern Amanda Symes, helped bring me into the twenty-first century with his social media expertise.

The people who wrote blurbs: Heid Erdrich, T.R. Hummer, Hilda Raz, and Brian Turner. Your thoughtful reading and enthusiasm for the book fill me with gratitude.

And above all, to my beloved spouse Jan, for believing in this project and in me. You had vision when I couldn't see my way through. You reminded me why these poems are important. This book, and my joy, wouldn't exist without you.

Many thanks to the editors of the following publications, where a number of these poems first appeared, sometimes in different versions:

"Uses for Salt" appeared in *Bellevue Literary Review*, Winter 2011.

"Rhubarb" appeared in *Vandal*, Fall/Winter 2012.

"Simples" appeared in *Ars Medica*, Fall 2012.

"Through My Window I See a Vision of My Mother," appeared in
    Barrow Street, December 2016.

"Orthography, 1895" appeared in *Women Poets Wearing Sweatpants*,
    January 2014.

"Some Rules for Teachers" appeared in *Floating Bridge Review*,
    Fall 2014.

"The Hired Man" appeared in *cahoodaloodaling*, Fall 2015.

"Sonata Beneath the Stars" appeared in *Postcard Poetry and Prose*,
    Winter 2016.

"Naming the Plants," "Hanging Tree," and "Thimble" appeared in
    Nimrod International Journal, Spring 2016.

"Present Fashions of Dress" and "We Gave Up" appeared in *Scoundrel
    Time,* Spring 2018.

"Bottle Gentian" appears in *Queer Nature*, forthcoming.

"The Hired Man" was nominated for a 2017 Pushcart Prize and Best of
    the Web award.

  The author gratefully acknowledges support
from Hedgebrook, Cornucopia Arts Council, the
Minnesota State Colleges and University system, the
National Endowment for the Humanities, and the
Minnesota State Arts Board in the completion of this manuscript.

KateLynn Hibbard is a fiscal 2012 recipient of an Artist Initiative
grant from the Minnesota State Arts Board. This activity is funded,
in part, by the Minnesota State Legislature from the State's arts and
cultural heritage fund with money from the vote of the people of
Minnesota on November 4, 2008.

ABOUT THE AUTHOR

Kate Lynn Hibbard's books include *Sleeping Upside Down* and *Sweet Weight*, and she edited *When We Become Weavers: Queer Female Poets on the Midwestern Experience*. Her honors include the Aestrea Foundation's Lesbian Writing Finalist Award, a McKnight Artist Fellowship in Poetry, two Minnesota State Arts Board Initiative Grants, a Jerome Foundation Travel Grant, and residencies at Hedgebrook and the Cornucopia Arts Council. A professor of writing and women's history at Minneapolis Community and Technical College, she lives with many pets and her spouse, Jan Arleth, in Saint Paul, Minnesota.

PHOTO BY LAURIE SCHNEIDER

HOWLING BIRD PRESS

Howling Bird Press is the book imprint of Augsburg University's Master of Fine Arts in Creative Writing program. Students enrolled in the publishing concentration, a two-semester course sequence, do the work of running the press, including editing, marketing, and fundraising, while studying the publishing profession and the book trade. The press sponsors an annual nationwide contest, which is judged by the student editors and senior faculty of the Creative Writing program. The press publishes the winning manuscript. The author receives a cash prize, book publication, distribution, and an invitation to read at the MFA program's summer residency in Minneapolis. The contest is open to manuscripts of poetry, fiction, and nonfiction on an alternating basis. *Simples*, by KateLynn Hibbard, is the winner of the 2018 Poetry Prize. Our previous books are *Still Life with Horses* by Jean Harper, winner of the 2017 Nonfiction Prize; *The Topless Widow of Herkimer Street* by Jacob M. Appel, winner of the 2016 Fiction Prize; and *At the Border of Wilshire & Nobody* by Marci Vogel, winner of the 2015 Poetry Prize. Howling Bird Press books are distributed by Small Press Distribution; they are available online and in bookstores nationwide.

Howling Bird Press wishes to acknowledge our editors Jannet Walsh, Sharon Sobotta, Colin Mustful, Diana Lopez Jones, Ciara Hall, Gabriel Benson, and our intern Amanda Symes. The press also thanks Augsburg's MFA faculty, mentors, and staff, including MFA Director Stephan Clark, Associate Director Lindsay Starck, professors Cary Waterman, Cass Dalglish, Heid E. Erdrich, and MFA Coordinator Kathleen Matthews. We thank English Department Chair Robert J. Cowgill and Augsburg President Paul Pribbenow. Special thanks to the supporters of the Howling Bird Press Publishing Fund, who—through Augsburg's Give to the Max campaign—provided generous support for this year's project, including Andrea Sanow, William Reichard and James Cihlar, Paul Pribbenow, Diana Lopez Jones, Judy Johnson, Douglas Green, Katherine Fagen, and Cass Dalglish.